Football is my life!

④ I play football and coach kids too.

The kids I coach can be very small!

It feels good to see them play!

In men's football you need a lot of skills. In women's football it is just the same. You need to mark and pass well, and to kick just as hard!

Boys can be a bit off with a woman coach and kick up a fuss. They can think we don't know as much as men!

But when I show the lads cool football skills, they are O.K. and keen to learn.

Girls are just as keen to learn, too.

A girl I coach is such a good player that she might be picked to play for Arsenal.

A mix of girls and boys in a team is good, if they are small.

But as they get bigger, teens need to be in 'all-girl' or 'all-boy' teams – as boys get too big and too tall for it to be a fair match.

All you need is a ball!
… So go for it!